A-Z OF TONGUE

Shameera Somani is an award-winning
interests include teaching children Elocution, Speech and Drama,
conducting workshops, designing health and educational content for
children and traveling. She volunteers for Aga Khan Health Board, India
and was a former Director of Aga Khan Health Service India. Her articles
on nutrition and healthy recipes have been published on
the.ismaili/nutrition centre website. Her travelogues have been published in
Corporate Tycoons magazine and on Corporate Tourism Website.

A-Z of Tongue Twisters

First Edition: November 2017

© Author

ISBN-10: 1979916926

ISBN -13: 978-1979916929

Createspace Independent Publishing Platform (27 November 2017)

Cover Design: Shameera Somani.

Clipart for Cover Design: Raspberry Smiley Openclipart

A-Z

OF

TONGUE TWISTERS

SHAMEERA SOMANI

ACKNOWLEDGEMENTS

For Rafiq, Aafiya and Rahin for being my sounding board and patiently listening to my tongue twisters and poems…

For Jeanette, Nishi and Mona my companions in our journey into the world of Speech, Drama and Elocution…

For Mom a source of strength and comfort…

For all the children I taught and on whom I tried and tested the tongue twisters…

PREFACE

A tongue twister is a series of words or sounds that are challenging to pronounce quickly and correctly when said in quick succession or sequence. They use alliteration which is the repetition of one sound. e.g. she sells sea shells on the seashore.

'A-Z of Tongue Twisters' is a delightful book that brings to you a complete range of tongue twisters in an alphabetical order. A section on poems with alliterations will intrigue and excite you. It also contains a section exclusively devoted to how to write tongue twisters. Word lists have been provided which will simplify the task of writing tongue twisters for beginners.

The book is suitable for all age groups and has a range of tongue twisters with varying levels of difficulty and ease of speaking. There are tongue twisters about friends and family members, birds and bees, people and places, feelings and emotions and very many things. Some are silly while others witty. Some are confusing while others are inspiring. There is a paucity of tongue twisters that are relevant and suitable to the Indian context and these have also been included to provide an Indian flavour. The range of tongue twisters will test your speaking skills, pronunciation and fluency and will also help in improving your vocabulary and diction.

These tongue twisters can enliven a party or a picnic, brush up pronunciation and diction skills of children in a speech, elocution or English language class. Families can have loads of fun writing, sharing and reciting tongue twisters on a lazy Sunday just like a game of chess or scrabble.

So, with a collection of tongue twisters to your rescue, it's time to tease and amuse your peers, confuse and connect with your family, impress and intimidate your colleagues, and get any and everyone truly tongue-tied.

Contents

SOME POPULAR TONGUE TWISTERS

1. Peter Piper picked a peck of pickled peppers
    A peck of pickled peppers Peter Piper picked
    If Peter Piper picked a peck of pickled peppers
    Where's the peck of pickled peppers Peter Piper picked?

2. Betty Botter bought some butter but the butter was bitter, so
    Betty bought some better butter to make the bitter butter
    better.

3. How much wood would a woodchuck chuck if a woodchuck
    could chuck wood?
    He would chuck, he would, as much as he could, and chuck
    as much wood
    As a woodchuck would if a woodchuck could chuck wood.

4. She sells seashells by the seashore.

5. I scream, you scream, we all scream for ice cream.

6. Fuzzy Wuzzy was a bear. Fuzzy Wuzzy had no hair.
    Fuzzy Wuzzy wasn't fuzzy, was he?

7. Can you can a can as a canner can can a can?

8. Red lorry, yellow lorry.

9. I slit the sheet, the sheet I slit, and on the slitted sheet, I
    sit.

10. A skunk sat on a stump and thunk the stump stunk, but
    the stump thunk the skunk stunk.

11. Don't trouble trouble, until trouble troubles you! If you
    trouble trouble triple trouble troubles you!

12. I saw Suzie sitting in a shoe shine shop.

13. When a doctor doctors a doctor, does the doctor doing the doctoring doctor as the doctor being doctored wants to be doctored or does the doctor doing the doctoring doctor as he wants to doctor?

14. I feel a feel, a funny feel, a funny feel I feel, if you feel the feel I feel, I feel the feel you feel.

A-Z OF TONGUE TWISTERS

A

Alisha and Arish eloped on an aeroplane to Argentina in April.

"Alone and lonely aren't alike," said aloof Aryaa to Alia.

Amar, Akbar and Anthony awkwardly asked Asha, Adaa and Annie for an antiseptic ointment to apply on their acne.

An army of ants attacked and ate the army's apples and avocados in August.

Angry Alibaba abducted anxious Abubaba in Abu Dhabi in April.

Angry Anita and anxious Alina ate apples and apricots all day in Allahabad.

Asters for stressed Ester on Easter to de-stress.

Aunty Anila was angry. Aunty Anila was anxious. Aunty Anila was in urgent need of an agony aunt for her ailment.

Ayra and Alia are always awake around eight a.m.

B

Bake and boil, braise and broil are but terms from a cookbook.

"Bake bread brown not black", blasted the beggar to the baker.

Bandits broke into the bank at daybreak and dumped the bag in the bonnet of the big, blue bus.

Beautiful blogger Belinda has a blog of books, birds and Broadway bands.

Bees, butterflies and bugs in the botanical gardens of Bangalore.

Bela bought brass bells and silver bells from Belgium for Bijal.

Bertha bought bats and balls, bells and boats for best friends Belinda and Bill.

Bertha broke the big, brown bowls by mistake.

Big bed bugs bit the big bums blue.

Big black boats sailed on the breezy blue bay.

Big boys made big bucks baking buns at the Bandra bakery.

Blisters on bums, fractures on fists, bugs in bellies bothered Belinda's brother.

Blue bus, red bus. Blue bus led the red bus.

Breta and Bela are besties forever.

Bring blue balloons and red balloons for the bored and bugged baboons.

Bring broccoli and Brussels sprouts, brinjals and butter for the barbecue brunch.

Bring bronze bowls and big blue bags from the big bazaar.

Broken bows, black bows. Rows of broken black bows.

Bullies bumped into Brian, so he had black and blue bruises and bumps on his belly.

Bunch of bananas, a bunch of keys but it's not a bunch of bees but a hive of bees.

Bunty went bungee jumping in Belgaum with Bijal.

Buzzing bumble bees bit Brijesh black and blue.

I can't bear to see the bored, big, bare bear.

The bakers did brisk business selling buns and burgers on the breezy blue bay.

There was a buzz in the bazaar as a bizarre bomb scare baffled the busy buyers.

C

Can the cans be canned by the canner? If the cans cannot be canned by the canner, then who will can the cans?

Can you catch a cough and cold by consuming cold coffee in the cold?

Cassim calmly canned the corns in the cans.

Centuries ago craftsmen chiseled and carved the contours in the caves.

Charlie chuckled and chirped for chillies in Chile.

Cheap chocolate chip cupcakes from Chinatown for Charmaine and Chirag.

Chetna chose a comfortable, cosy corner of the class to chew on Cheddar cheese.

Chicken and chips, coke and Choco lava cake for Chrysler's christening.

Chris was christened on Christmas in Kolkatta.

Cinnamon cakes and lemonade drinks for a cent.

Credit cards and cash for cars, crystals and clothes.

Creepy crawlies couldn't be counted by curious Colin correctly.

Creepy crawlies like crickets and cockroaches crept curiously in Candy's car and drove her crazy.

Crisp, crunchy chips and choco flakes.

Cups and clips, soups and slips, scents and spirits sold for a steal at the sale.

Cyberbullies cheated Sherly in a cyber café in Chennai.

How many cans can a canner can, if a canner can can cans?

Is this the chewy child who chewed on chillies, not cherries?

Not a clue why the crew couldn't cruise along the coast.

The common man's commonness is uncommon. So, is the common man a common man or an uncommon common man?

What would Charlie choose? Cheap cheese, shrimp chips, or chocolate chips?

A cello tape?
A sticky cello tape?
Sticky cello tapes are out of stock.
Stick with sticky glue instead.

A cook bought a book.

Look at the book the cook bought.
Is it a cookbook that the cook bought?
If it isn't a cookbook that the cook bought
Then where is the book that the cook bought?

Chris crossed a criss- cross crossing.
Kors crossed a criss-cross crossing.
Is the criss-cross crossing that Chris crossed the same criss-cross
crossing that Kors crossed?
If it is, then did Chris and Kors criss-cross each other at the criss-
cross crossing?

If a cauldron could cook cod,
How much cod
Would a cauldron cook,
If a cauldron could cook cod?

The chef chops chips.
The chef shopped for cheap chipped chocolates.
The chef chopped cheap chipped chocolates into chips.

D

A dessert in a desert is well deserved when stressed.

Daddy ordered a dozen, delicious doughnuts for darling Deena and
dreamy Diana.

Daddy's delighted to dine with his doting daughter.

Daisy daily daydreams in her dormitory of devils and Dracula in
dungeons.

Dick doodled ducks and drakes for the dukes.

Did dashing Danish take dainty Dina on a date to Delhi in December?

Did dumb Dora wash her dainty doll in the dishwasher?

Dim sums for dumb Dimple for a dollar.

Dina doll doesn't do that dare for a dollar, dear.

Diya decorated a dozen dazzling diyas for Diwali.

Dosas for Disha and idlies for Daddy from the Delhi deli.

Double Decker bus, for double rides and double the dollars.

Dreamy Dolly drew dolls and dragons on the dashboard.

I dream a dream, a daring dream, a daring dream I dream. If you dream the dream I dream, I dream the dream you dream.

If my dad's dad is my granddad. If my dad is my son's granddad. Then whose granddad, am I?

The dude went on a blind date with a dame. The dumb dude dated the deaf dame. Their senseless date doomed and ended in a disaster.

Would you dare to dance with a dangerous dragon in the dark dungeons in December?

E

Eighteen electric eels for eight eager eagles.

Ellie the elephant is the eldest of eleven elephants that Elba enjoys imitating.

Ettan ate Easter eggs in England eagerly.

Eventually, everyone is extremely excited about everything.

Everybody expressed their emotions elegantly and eloquently.

Extravagant expenses eluded economical Edgar.

"What exactly is an excellent education?" enquired Ed to Edgar.

Why exactly does Elizabeth enjoy eating enormous eggs every day?

F

A flock of flamingoes flew far away on Friday at four.

Fake photos of Farida were found on her friend's Facebook on Friday. How will Farida face her friends from now on?

Fat feet. Flat feet. Fat flat feet.

Feroz found frozen French fries in his fridge and fried them for his five friends on Friday.

Fight for your rights! Is it right to fight?

Fiona was a foodie who fed on few leftovers for free.

First find the five funny finger rings from the fish pool, you fool.

Fish fries and fresh, fried fish for Friday's fun fiesta.

Five blue fish fled from four red fish in the fish pool.

Five flies, four fleas, few fireflies flew far away.

Five frantic phone calls for finding Fanny.

Flora fetched farm fresh fruits for forty-five francs in France.

Flowers red, flowers blue. A basketful or few flowers for you?

"Forever and frequently finding faults with friends isn't funny", fumed Fanny.

Forgive and forget. How can you forget to forgive and forget? I can't forgive you for forgetting to forgive.

Four fairies feared the five elves.

Four fashionable females wearing flip flops and frilly frocks flocked to the fashion show.

Four, fat friends flew to Finland in February and fed on few flatbreads.

Four fathers fought forever. The four fathers were our forefathers.

Four fire engines fought the flaring flames.

Four fishermen fishing for fat, fresh fish in February found female frocks funnily instead.

Four footballers followed the fellow who fled with their footballs.

Four former foes forged friendship on Facebook.

Four former friends are now foes forever.

Four frogs and five fish who were friends are now foes.

Fresh fruits from farm to fork.

From fat to fit, fast fast and forget to feast.

The famished families finally filled themselves with fish fillet.

The frying pan flew from the foolish fool's fist.

G

A gaggle of geese grew up in the green grasslands.

A giver gives not gets. Are you a giver or a getter? It is greater to give than to get.

Garima gazed from the glass, as the grey goats grazed greedily on the green grass.

Get a grater for Geeta to grate the gourds.

Gia and Gita got gathia and jalebis from Gujarat.

Ginger and garlic ground and grated into a gravy for granny and Janie.

Give grape juice and ginger ale to Gladys and gang.

Go get green grass in a clean, green glass.

Good blood, bad blood. Red blood, blue blood.

'Google up glutton', said giggling Greta to greedy Govind.

Great-grandma Gauri graciously greets her great-grandkids, Gita and Greta.

Grumpy, greedy gorillas grabbed the grapes and greens.

The greedy gang grabbed the gadgets and gizmos.

H

A hedge, a hog but not a hedgehog.

A hissing snake bit Humpty's horse and the horse cried hoarse and died.

Hamburgers for Henry and big burgers for hungry beggars.

Henry, are you hungry in Hungary? Hurry lets hog on some hamburgers!

Hotcakes, home baked for hungry hogs.

How many cakes would a baker bake if a baker could bake cakes?

How many hungry horses can be fed by hundred haystacks?

How much hope can a hopeless, helpless hoper hope for to be happy?

Hurrah! It's a holiday for Holi in Haryana.

The hunter who hunted became the hunted.

I

An interest in internet is an interesting interest, indeed. Isn't it?

Ice cubes and ice creams for Ilyan and Iliana.

Ira and Ila fell ill and took a pill in Ireland.

Is this the icebox that Isha bought? If this is not the icebox Isha bought, then where is the icebox that Isha bought?

Is this the island I can sail to from India easily?

J

A jade for Jane and Greta gets a garnet.

A jumbo jet, a jigsaw puzzle, a jumper suit is what Jane gifted Jill on her June birthday.

Don't judge people even though people judge you because if you judge people what's the difference between people and you.

Jalapenos for Gisele, gherkins for Gladys, zucchinis for Janice.

Jams and jellies jiggled as the girls giggled.

Jiya and Zoya had jam biscuits with ginger ale at the Japanese zoo.

Joggers jogged at the joggers' park in Juhu in January.

Jokers, jugglers, joggers and jockeys did a jig at the gig.

Jolly Jolly joked and jumped at the girly gig.

Juggle balls, juggle bells, juggle all the way. The jugglers are coming to juggle balls and bells away.

Julie and Zina visited zoos and jungles in June and July.

Jumping Jack, juggling jugglers and giggling Jiggy joked and gestured on a jumbo jet.

K

How much does kind Kashmira care for quiet Cavery, not even quiet Cavery cares to know.

Keya was keen to see Neel kneel now.

Kittens and cats came to the college canteen in Kolkata for cutlets and kebabs.

Koalas and kangaroos came calmly to Karen in Queensland.

L

A lawyer can be a liar, but not all lawyers are liars neither are all liars lawyers.

A little love and loads of laughter with lady love is lots of luck.

Lace and leather look lovely together.

Larry applied lemon liniment to his limping right limb.

Larry saw a red lorry loaded with blueberries and raspberries.

Leeches under bridges. Bridget under bridges. Leeches on Bridget and bridges.

Lily lisps and limps. Her lips lisp and her legs limp leading to many slips.

Lily loves berries and lilacs but not cherries and lilies.

Lip gloss and lipsticks for lovely luscious lips.

Lisa and Raisa were laughing out loud in their room in Rome.

Little Lina lifted lazy Lionel lovingly.

Looks like Lidia loves her long locks more than her long frocks.

Lots of lollipops for Papa and Lola.

Luv loved to live, laugh, love until his love, Liz lied and left him in a lurch.

Take a loaf of bread and a lump of cake to eat at the lake.

The lovely lady longingly looked at the lad who loved some other lass.

M

How many misses missed the mystery movie on Monday?

Magicians magically made mice move in midair majestically.

Many are mesmerized by the mystery of the melancholic moments in moonlit nights.

Many men make mistakes by marrying misses in Mississippi.

May Mary marry Larry and be merry.

Mickey and Minnie mouse loved mousse that melted in their mouths.

Mischievous Mrinmai munched messily on mangoes mostly on Mondays in May.

Miserable Molly was mum as she had measles and mums on Monday morning.

Miss Molly married a millionaire in Milan on a Monday morning in May.

Mittens for kittens who meet Miss Meeta in kitchens.

Mohan's mobile had mysterious messages and missed calls from very many misses.

Mold, mildew, moss mess with Miss Moss's immunity.

Mona likes muskmelons and marshmallows the most.

More money, more worry, no money, so worry.

Musa and Myra mimicked their mom merrily on Monday.

Mushrooms for Seema and marshmallows for Meesha.

Mushy marshmallows melt in the mouth.

My mom's mom is my grandmom, and her mom is my great grandmom.

Mysterious mermaids mimed, murmured and mimicked in the moonlight.

The military marched on a Monday in March to Morocco.

The mixer mixes the spices to a mixed spice mixture.

Very many misses missed being missus because they refused to be kissed when they were misses.

N

A new knife for a new wife is not good for your life.

All night naughty Naina knitted with knitting needles a neat net for natty Nishi.

Natty Nita noted the notice that neither Tina nor Nia noticed.

Naughty Neela knows nothing new, but she knows that she knows nothing new.

Neither Nida nor Numa knew anything of the nuisance in their neighbourhood until they noticed it on the news.

Never say never. If you ever have to say never just be clever and say no instead of never.

"Nice to see neat, knitted knickers for a nickel", noted Nikhil.

Nitty had knitting needles to knit nets. The nets have knots. Now she will need new knitting needles to knit new nets without knots.

No one knows what the nun knows. Do you think the nun knows what she thinks she knows, and no one knows?

No, no I don't know what you want to know? Does anybody know what he wants to know, now?

Nobody knows why naughty Noddy nodded at the nice nun at noon.

No wife, no life.
New wife, new life.
Know wife, know life.

No woman no worry.

More women more worry.

Numerous rumours were murmured by humorous Romeo.

O

An octopus, an oyster in the ocean isn't odd.

Olga ordered onions, oysters, olives, oregano and oranges online.

Orange orangutans ate orange oranges in October.

Owls hooted all night outdoors in Ooty.

The officer offered to offer an offering and ordered oranges often.

P

A posse of policemen paraded and posed for pictures in Puducherry.

Pass the pickled pumpkins, please.

Patty painted the pots. Polly purchased plenty of plants. Polly planted the plants in the pots that Patty painted.

People picked plum pudding and pumpkin pies for a pound.

People post plenty of pictures of high pixels on plenty of platforms.

Peter passes the pepper and paper to Paul patiently and perfectly.

Phil flicked the fudge from the fridge.

Pick some poky pineapples, with purple passion fruits and plump plums for the picnic.

Pickled peppers packed in pickle jars, for a pound.

Pink purses and pant pockets full of pennies and paisa.

Pinky proved the problem was problematic.

Pins prick painfully on palms.

Pizza and pasta, pudding and pie packed for Paul's party.

Please, pause for a cause and pay and pray.

"Please, place the prose paper properly", pleaded the prince to Rose.

Plump Pandas played in the pool to be cool.

Plump Pappu picked a pipe and played with it on the picnic.

Polly the playful parrot picked and pricked the pungent peppers.

Poor Peter the potter, painted his pots and plates purple and pink.

Popular Priya played the piano patiently.

Pretty Pinky playfully posed for plenty of pictures in Paris.

Pretty Polly played with pink pigs on the picnic.

Pretty, petty Priya had perpetual, persistent problems with her peers.

Prisha paid a penny for purple periwinkles and pink primroses.

Push and pull the play dough to make plenty of pretty pots and plates.

The pastor patiently preached on the perils and problems of the poor.

The patient patiently waited for pills for his chills. But the bill made the patient patient impatient and shrill.

The prince and pauper paused to pose for pictures in Patiala.

What a pity? Pluto is no longer a planet and people aren't too pleased.

"What is the password for Paula's P.C.?" pleaded Priya.

Q

Quasar and Koreen quarreled over the quality and quantity of coats.

Quietly but quickly queue for the quills and quilts from Queensland.

Quietly the queen quilted the quilts.

Quitters quit questioning the questions that quiz them.

The quaint queen was quiet when questioned about her quarrel with the quintessential drama queen.

The quiet queen quit keeping quills and quilts.

The quiet queen quit questioning and quizzing the quitters.

R

In rains, rivers rise and ravage the riverside and roads recklessly.

Please try to remember remember. If you remember remember, say remember. If you don't remember remember, say don't remember. Will you remember remember or should I remind you to remember remember?

Raul lavished ravishing Ruby with red ruby rings.

Ravishing Lavina loved red roses and struck some poses with Raveena.

Reclusive Romeo rejected the roses from his repentant, lost lover Rose.

Red bangles, green bangles. So many bangles made of brass and glass.

Red roses for winners and faded roses for losers.

Red rubbers, red ribbons. Yellow rubbers, yellow ribbons.

Remember the name of the member who remembered the members' names.

Remember, Lola, roamed in Rome alone?

Right, write or write right. What is right?

Roma rolled a roller. Lola rolled a roller. Roma and Lola rolled a round roll lower.

Rows of roses and laces for ladies.

Ryan is a voracious reader. Lion is a ferocious eater. Books and flesh were fodder for Ryan and lion.

The right light is lighter than the left light. Right?

S

A sheep met a sheep and there were two sheep.
Two sheep met two sheep and they were sheep too.
Four sheep were minced in a shop and they were sheekh kebabs.

A sheet in a pit. A pit with a sheet. A sheet in a pot. A pot with a sheet.

A sheet in a pit. A slitted sheet in a pit. A slitted sheet shut the pit.

A shirt I stitched. I stitched a shirt. Upon a stitched shirt I sat still.

A simple silver souvenir for single Sally from Switzerland.

A single silver ring, for the single sisters Serina and Selina?

A silver sliver for Cinderella's silver slipper.

A straight line. A square slate. A straight line on a square slate.

I saw sheep, a ship I saw, upon a ship I sailed with sheep.

I see sheep. A ship I see. I see a ship full of sheep.

Is selfish Sheela sharing her sweet sherbet in summer with stubborn Sailesh?

Sachin scored a century thanks to the six sixes he struck.

Salim is spooked by slithering snakes and scary scorpions.

Salman slyly sold his six sheep to the sick sheikh.

Sand, sea and sun are for all to see in summer.

Serve a sunny side up to Sunny on Sundays.

Seven, single sisters in skirts and shirts served sweets and shrimps to seven sailors in shirts and shorts.

She saw shiny ships at the seashore on Sunday.

She sells shoes and socks for a shilling at the seashore.

She shopped shamelessly for shoes, stoles, skirts and shirts at the sale!

She shows silk stoles to the shoppers at the stall.

She stood shattered as he slaughtered the sheep.

Shiny, silver, silk, scarves are for sale on Sundays in summer.

Shoes, slippers, socks and stockings are selling at so many shops.

Should Suchi send sushi or shellfish for Suzie on Saturday?

Should Suzie shut the shoe shop at the seaside at sunset in summers?

Shy Seema and sly Sheila stole seven, silk slips from the shops on Saturday.

Silk shirts and satin skirts swiftly sold at the small shop.

Silly Shelina showed her selfie with Shekhar to selfish Serina.

Silly, scary scarecrows scared the crows and crowds away.

Simple Simon stole the sheets from the stationary shop.

Simran saw the spider and shirked and shivered all of Saturday.

Six Sikhs shared the shrimps and soup with seven sheikhs on Sunday.

Six soggy socks and seven smelly shoes.

Sixty-six sheep sleep on slopes and hills.

Slowly but surely, she shall succeed someday.

Slowly sail the ships from the seashore.

Slurping sticky, sweet sherbet through straws.

Smart Shanaya and shy Sanaya sang a simple song for the school show in Shimla.

So many socks, shoes, stockings and sandals are selling at seaside shops on Sunday.

Soles for shoes and soups for souls.

Some Sundays seem so slow and long and others so swift and short.

Someday someone will surely show me some simple sums to solve.

Sometimes Samar, summersaults in the summer.

Sometimes Sheila simply sings silly songs slowly on Sundays.

Soon the sun shall set in the sea.

Sow some seeds in summer and sew some socks for winter.

Summer season is a reason for some sea and sun.

Susan has a passion for fashion.

Swiftly and silently the snake slithered on the seashore.

The sheikh savoured the sheekh kebabs on the seashore in Sharjah.

The shops shutters shut sharp at six on Sundays.

T

A tired traveller has tears as he nears the end of the travels and trails.

A traveller travelled to Timbuktu.
A traveller travelled to Kathmandu.
The two travellers travelled from Timbuktu to Kathmandu or from Kathmandu to Timbuktu?

One tooth is a tooth; two are teeth but what about the tiny toddler who has no teeth? Is he toothless or has he teeth less?

Take three, tasty tacos for the two, trendy teenagers.

Ten tiny, tender twigs to twist and twirl.

Ten tuskers trumpeted triumphantly as they trampled the tiger.

Terribly tiring Tuesday for the teachers who taught trigonometry to terrified teenagers.

Terrifying tales about tiger trails are on T.V. on Tuesday's at twilight.

The tailor tailored two T-shirts for the twins to take on a travel trail.

The tantrums of toddlers and terrible teenagers are transient troubles.

The teacher who taught the cheater is feeling cheated because the cheater cheated.

The teachers taught the toddlers to twist and twirl today.

The tiger trailed the tiny, timid tortoise at twilight.

The trouble with trouble is that it doesn't trouble you until you trouble it, so stay out of trouble with trouble.

Three teddy bears tumbled on the two trampolines today.

Tia and Tisha, the tiny twins, tossed and turned ten thousand times tonight.

Tia tasted tangy tamarind and tangerines on a trek in Turkey.

Tia took two tickets of ten thousand on Tuesday, for a trip to Turkey.

Tiger's torso had a terrifying tiger's tattoo that he tweeted on Tuesday.

Tights with tunics, pants with pleats for pretty Tina.

Tina tweeted about the tornado tragedy two times on Tuesday.

Tiny Thumbelina was taken to Timbuktu by the terrible troll on Thursday.

Tips and hints to paint shades and tints.

Tisha tweeted about travel trips' tips.

Tring tring rang the telephone twice on Tuesday at two.

Two thieves stole a topaz and a turquoise in Tokyo tonight.

Two times ten is twenty and twenty times thousand is twenty thousand.

Two times two is not twenty-two.

U

I understand that you don't understand what I understand but understand that not everything and everyone can be understood. Did you understand?

I utterly understood the utterances of Uncle Arthur.

Uncle Usman's umbrellas were under the oven.

Undies of my buddies are under the teddies.

Usha ushered the United States guests.

V

Very many wandering, weary visitors visited Varanasi wondering what to do.

Victoria said the verse while Veronica played the violin.

Vinegars and wines for visitors in Valencia.

Visitors were very wary when they went to Venice.

W

How many wishes would you wish, if a wicked witch asked you to wish?

Warp and weft, woollen or worsted, wondered the weaver as he wove vests and waistcoats.

Wear warm woollies to warm you in winters.

Weavers wove woollen and worsted vests for workers to wear.

What a wonderful world it is! I wonder what this wonderful world would be if it wasn't as wonderful as it is.

What will Willi wish if he wins? Let him win to wish.

What will wishers wish if they were to wish for a wish?

"When will wars wind up", wondered wary Wanda.

When will Willi and Wonka varnish the wind chimes?

"When will women's woes vanish?" wondered Waheeda.

Where is the watch that William wanted to wear on Wednesday to the wedding?

Which watch would you watch if you were to watch a watch?

Why was the winter wind so windy on Wednesday?

Why were there wriggling worms in Veronica's vest?

Why would the woodpecker peck on woods in winters for worms, when there are not very many worms in winter?

Wild wolves wandered in the whistling woods. Would you venture in the woods to watch the wandering wild wolves?

Will Wilma wed William on Wednesday in Vienna?

Wilma wound the watch which she wore on Wednesday.

Wise women win wars with words, not swords.

Wonder what the vicar said to the wizard on Wednesday?

Y

Yellow yachts sailed for the youngsters of Yorkshire.

Yellow yolks for those young fellows.

Yellow yo-yos for those jolly fellows.

You were young when you yearned for yo-yos.

Z

The zippers jammed in my zebra striped jacket even though I tried zillion times.

Zealously they zipped the Jaguars over the zebra crossing.

Zebras and Jaguars are to be seen at the Zanzibar zoo.

Zeenat and Jeanette saw zebras and giraffes at the Jaipur zoo in June.

Zinnias and gerberas joyfully jigged in June.

Zombies jumped and zoomed over the jamboree in the jungle.

Zucchini and gherkins were eaten zestfully by the Zulus.

POEMS

A Malady
Anemia and bulimia.
Measles and mums.
Diarrhea and dengue.
A malady for many
And a tragedy for some.

Berries in Bellies
Blue berries and mulberries,
Raspberries and strawberries,
Gooseberries and blackberries,
Very, many berries in big bellies.

Bubblegum
Bubblegum blue,
Bubblegum red,
Double bubblegum.
Double the bubbles.

Birthday
Bela brought in her birthday at the beaches.
Balloons and bouquets bought by besties
Beena, Babloo, Bhavna and Benji.
Brunching on bhelpuri, bhajias and pav bhaji.
Birthday bumps were given by the boys.
Gifts of books, bags and beautiful toys.

Christmas
Baby Jesus was born in Bethlehem
Which is the gem of Jerusalem.
Christmas time is coming closer

So, stick your stockings sooner.
Santa on a sleigh in a sweater
Ridden by Rudolph the reindeer.
Christmas carols and
Choirs in churches.
Trees with tinkling bells and baubles
Chocolate cakes, candies and candles.
The midnight mass no one can miss.
Oh! The charisma of Christmas.

Damsel in Distress

Dainty Dina the darling of her Daddy.
Went on a date with dashing Danny.
He promised her diamonds, dollars and dirhams.
Delighted she said, 'I do' and was on the run.
They married and eloped to Dubai in December.
They lodged in a dingy room and got some slumber.
Soon the dame was cooking dinners and doing dishes.
While the dude was drinking which was against her wishes.
Dina's life was on the brink of disaster.
As for Danny he was doomed hereafter.
The Damsel in distress was dejected but not defeated.
She phoned her Daddy and stressed to be rescued.
Daddy with a dozen bouncers dashed to Dubai.
And rescued Dina who left without even a goodbye.

Diwali

Daddy lights a dozen decorative diyas.
Leena lights the lamps and lanterns.
Rewa draws rangolis using red, rose colour.
Tiny Tisha puts torans at the entrance door.
Mummy makes many mithais to munch.
Poojas by Panditji followed by lunch.

Boom, bang! Burst the bombs in the bylanes.
The sound of firecrackers is louder than airplanes.
Ram ruined Ravan, the devil.
Diwali is victory of good over evil.

Eid

The feasting follows the fast.
The moon was sighted at last.
Mubarak! Mubarak! muttered Shama.
"Eid is here so take your eidi" announced Abba.
Ammi made mithais and mutton biryani.
Meher and Mehak applied marvelous mehendi.
Nawaz and Nadeem said the namaz in the masjid.
The mohalla was abuzz with songs of Sajid and Wajid.

Pajamas

Pink Pajamas,
Purple pajamas,
Paisley printed pajamas,
Pin stripped pajama,
Plentiful pajamas to pounce and play in.

Remedies for Maladies

Bruises and blisters,
Fractures and fissures,
Bandages and plasters,
Ointments and liniments,
A remedy for every malady.

Rafiq the Runner

Rafiq, the runner ran terrific races.
Everyone raved and ranted,
"Run Rafiq run!"

What was he running for?
Who was he running from?
Who was he running after?
Who was he running with?
Numerous humorous rumours
spread faster than the races he ran.

Sea Side

Sea, sand and seashells.
Swimsuits, shorts and shades.
Pails, shovels and some spades.
Hair tied up in buns and braids.
Silk sarongs and sunscreen lotion.
Snorkeling and scuba diving in slow motion.
Smoothies and shakes to sip and slurp.
Shrimps and snacks to swallow and burp.
Shops and stalls are slowly shutting.
Time to say sayonara as the sun is setting.

The Teacher or Cheater?

A teacher went to a teacher training school.
She wanted to be taught how to teach.
A teacher taught the teacher.
The teacher thought the teacher was terrible.
Which teacher was terrible?
The one who was trying to teach the teacher
Or the one who was taught by the teacher.
At last, it was time for the terminals.
The teacher carried a chit in her windcheater.
The teacher caught the teacher with a chit cheating.
Soon the teacher was teased.
The teacher is a cheater!
The cheater is a teacher!!

Woodcutter and Wiseman

A woodcutter wept in the woods.
He was worried and had a tale of woes.
He wished for a wife, wealth and wine.
A Wiseman watched the woodcutter whine.
"A wishing well or a well-wisher.
What would you wish, if you had to wish?
Wish wisely!", warned the Wiseman.

A GUIDE TO WRITING TONGUE TWISTERS

What is a tongue twister? A tongue twister is a series of words or sounds that are challenging to pronounce quickly and correctly when said in quick succession or sequence. They use alliteration which is the repetition of one sound. E.g. she sells sea shells on the seashore.

Alliterations in tongue twisters: Alliteration is a literary device in which similar sounding consonants are used in succession. Hence there is repetition of beginning sounds of words. Please note that alliteration is about sounds and should not be confused with letters.

The letters **C** (Cinderella) and **S** (Simon) both make the '**s**' sound.

The letters **K** (kite) and **C** (cow) make the '**c**' sound.

The letter **F** (foe) and **Ph** (phone) both make the '**f**' sound.

The letters **G** (giraffe) and **J** (jackal) both sometimes make the '**j**' sound.

The letter **N** (new), **Gn** (gnu), **Kn** (knew) make the 'n' sound

The letter **R** (right) and **Wr** (write) both make the '**r**' sound.

The letter **S** (scent) and **C** (cent) both sometimes make the '**s**' sound.

The letters **Y** (you) and **U** (use) and **Eu** (Europe) make the '**u**' sound.

The letters **Z** (zebra) and **X** (Xulu) make the '**z**' sound.

A point to be emphasized is that the to be called an alliteration words need not be consecutively next to each other in the sentence (although more often than not they are).

How to write tongue twister: Let's begin with something easy and then with practice you will be able to move on to more challenging ones.

1. Choose a letter from A-Z. As beginners avoid the letters Q, X, Y, Z as they are difficult.
2. Next write names of people, places and things beginning with the letter. E.g. 'M'- Mary, mango, Mumbai.
3. Now think of describing words/adjectives beginning with the letter and note them down. E.g. merry, mischievous, marvellous and so on.
4. Next, think of some doing words/ verbs beginning with the letter. Mimed, mimicked, moved, made, munched, etc.
5. Also note if there are any numbers, days of the week or months beginning with the letter. E.g. May, Monday.
6. Now using these words write a tongue twister. E.g. Mary ate mangoes in May.
7. Now edit your tongue twister and see if it can be made richer. E.g. Merry Mary munched on mangoes in May.
8. Lastly look at it one more time, can be it be tweaked if too long or expanded if short. Read it aloud and check how it sounds. You may also want to share it with family and friends and take a feedback. Make necessary changes. Your tongue twister is now ready.

    E.g. Merry Mary munched on many mangoes mostly on Mondays in May.

Tips on writing tongue twisters: Here are some tips and hints that will be helpful when writing tongue twisters.
1. Make word lists beginning with different letters of the alphabet. These come in handy while writing tongue twisters. A thesaurus and dictionary will be useful. Word lists have been provided in the book, but you may want to add more to the list or make lists of your own.
2. Play around with the commonly confused sounds where most people fumble and stutter.
    - **'sh'**, **'s'** sound. 'she' is mispronounced as 'see'!

- '**j**',' **z**' sound. 'Zee T.V.' is mispronounced as 'Jee T.V.'.
- '**th**', '**d**' sound. 'thunder' in a hurry sounds as 'dunder'!
- '**r**',' **l**' sound. 'roller' in haste is mispronounced as 'loller'!

3. Repetition, rhyme and rhythm work wonders for tongue twisters.
   - Red bus. Blue bus. Red bus led the blue bus.
   - More money, more worry, no money, so worry.

4. Homonyms (words that are pronounced the same and spelt the same but have different meanings) and homophones (words that are pronounced the same and have different spellings and different meanings) make tongue twisters very witty and interesting.
   - How many cans can a canner can if a canner can can cans?
   - I see a sea, a sea I see.

5. Select topics that are of current interest or that have an element of wisdom, humour, wit and perhaps are even vane and silly.
   - No wife, no life.
     New wife, new life.
     Know wife, know life.

6. Be original and think out of the box. How about writing a tongue twister poem, or a question as a tongue twister?
   - Will Wilma wed William on Wednesday in Vienna?

7. Be patient and practice. With time you will soon be an ace at them.

8. Keep a pen and notepad handy. You never know when and where you may be inspired to write a tongue twister.

Use the graphic organizer template to write words with the same letter/ sound. You can then use some or all the words to make a sentence. Edit the sentence and your tongue twister is ready.

Tongue Twister Graphic Organiser Template:

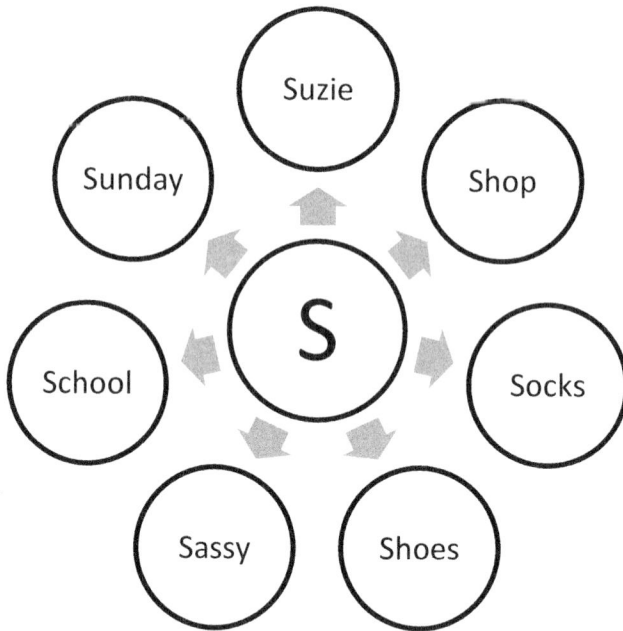

Tongue Twister: **Sassy Suzie sells school socks and shoes at the shop on Sunday.**

Possibilities of using tongue twisters: Tongue twisters are for all: the young and the old, men, women and children. They can be used as speech exercises in a phonics or a speech and elocution class. They help us to speak clearly with proper diction and pronunciation. With patience and practice, they improve fluency and accent. We learn new words and our vocabulary increases as similar sounding words can have very different meanings. They can be used as fillers to brighten up a long dry session in schools, colleges or offices. Parties and gatherings come alive with tongue twisters. Families can have loads of fun writing, sharing and reciting tongue twisters on a lazy Sunday just like a game of chess or scrabble. Long journeys while travelling, getting bored and not knowing what to do are all opportunities for tongue twisters. The possibilities are limitless.

Topics for tongue twisters:

1. **Animals and birds:** Ever wondered what differentiates man from other animals? It's his brains. So now wrack your brains and write some tongue twisters on animals and birds. The sounds animals make, the striking features they have, the collective nouns used to describe groups of animals are some ideas you may want to include while writing tongue twisters.
   - Big, bed bugs bit the big bums blue.
   - Ellie the elephant is the eldest of eleven elephants that Elba enjoys imitating.
   - A flock of flamingoes flew far away.

2. **Family, friends and foes:** Why not write tongue twisters about your family members. Dotting dads and marvellous mummies, silly sisters and bossy brothers, agony aunts and uninvited uncles, curious cousins, noisy nephews and nice nieces, generous grandpas and gracious grandmas, harassed husbands and worried wives. How can nosy neighbours be left behind?
   Do not forget the friends who turned foes and foes that turned friends. Friends who are enemies or enemies who are friends whom we call frenemies! How about writing one for your BFF? Best Friend/s Forever.
   - Four, former friends are now foes forever.
   - Daddy ordered a dozen, delicious doughnuts for darling Deena and dainty Diana.
   - No wife no life.
     New wife new life.
     Know wife know life.

3. **Fruits, flowers and vegetables:** How about writing a tongue twister about your favourite fruit, vegetable or flower?

    -   Blue berries and mulberries,
        Raspberries and strawberries,
        Very, many berries in big bellies.
    -   Zucchini and gherkins were eaten zestfully by the Zulus.
    -   Pick some poky pineapples, with purple passion fruits and plump plums for the picnic.
    -   Prisha paid a penny for purple periwinkles and pink primroses.

4. **Celebrations and occasions:** Life is a celebration. Imagine what it would be like without occasions and celebrations. Tongue twisters for birthdays, anniversaries, baby showers. Diwali, Eid, Christmas, Holi, Easter, New year are but some of the festivals for fun and frolic. How about writing some tongue twisters on these?

    -   Chicken and chips, coke and Choco lava cake for Chrysler's christening.
    -   Hurrah! It's a holiday for Holi in Haryana.
    -   Diya bought a dozen decorative diyas in Diwali.

5. **Feelings and Emotions:** Smile and the world smiles with you. Weep and you weep alone. Our moods, feelings and emotions, as well as those of the people around us, influence our day to day lives. Express your thoughts, feelings and ideas through tongue twisters.

    -   Everybody enjoyed expressing their emotions elegantly and eloquently.
    -   Eventually, everyone is extremely excited about everything.

- Angry Alibaba abducted anxious Abubaba in Abu Dhabi in April.

6. **People, professions and places:** We meet all sorts of people every day. Some are funny while others are a nuisance or serious. Some are simple while others are silly. Observe the people you meet in your daily life, it could be the baker, barber, butcher or blackmailer! Writing some tongue twisters on them would be fun. Politicians, page three celebrities, film stars are another breed which can be used as feed when you write tongue twisters.

   The world is now a global village with so many places that have been seen and waiting to be explored from Timbuktu to Katmandu. It's a small world after all. Go on let the creative juices flow.
   - Dashing Dino dated dainty Dina in December in Damascus.
   - Four fishermen fishing for fat, fresh fish in February found female frocks funnily instead.
   - The bakers did brisk business selling buns and burgers on the breezy blue bay.

7. **Everyday objects:** We are always looking at things and objects in shops and stores, roads and homes. They could be clothes, stationary items, furniture, equipment, gizmos and gadgets. Get on your thinking caps and hunt for some more.
   - Blue bus,
     Red bus.
     Blue bus led the red bus.

8. **Nature:** Wondering what to write a tongue twister about? Look for inspiration in nature. There are many reasons to write tongue twisters about nature, not just seasons, sun,

sand, sea, beaches, forests, jungles, dessert and mountains. The sky is the limit.

- Sand, sea and sun are for all to see in summer.
- In rains, rivers rise and ravage the riverside and roads recklessly.

9. **Questions:** Sometimes tongue twisters can be questions which could be silly, confusing, rhetorical or funny. What, why, when, where and how with the letters W and H lend themselves easily to questions as tongue twisters.

- **What:** What will wishers wish if they were to wish for a wish?
- **When:** "When will women's woes vanish?" wondered Wanda.
- **Why:** Why was the winter wind so windy on Wednesday?
- **Where:** Where is the watch that William wanted to wear on Wednesday to the wedding?
- **Which:** Which watch would you watch if you were to watch a watch?
- **How:** How much hope can a hopeless, helpless hoper hope for?

10.**Fantasy:** Fantasies fascinate/d all of us. Characters from fantasy are a fantastic idea for tongue twisters. Fairies and elves, goblins and giants, mermaids and trolls, dragons and Dracula, demons and devils.

- Four fairies feared the five elves.
- Mysterious mermaids mimed, murmured and mimicked mostly on Mondays.
- Would you dare to dance with a dangerous dragon in the dark dungeons in December?

11.Virtual world: With the advent of computers and the social media life has never been the same. With them came their own distinct terminologies and jargon.

- 'Google up glutton', said giggling Greta to greedy Govind.
- Fake photos of Farida were found on her friend's Facebook on Friday. How will Farida face her friends from now on?
- Tiger's torso had a terrifying tiger's tattoo that he tweeted on Tuesday.

12. Everything and anything: Yes, you can write tongue twisters about everything and anything or at least some things. Start right now.

How to recite a tongue twister: The proof of the pudding lies in its eating so also the proof of a good tongue twister lies in its recitation. You can challenge someone to recite it quickly or repeatedly. Tongue twisters could also be coloured with various emotions. The same tongue twister can be recited angrily, sadly, happily, enviously, as a surprise and so on. Also in a game, you could dare someone to recite a tongue twister like a character e.g. toddler, old person, robot, king, beggar, a rock star, etc. Voice modulation is important while reciting tongue twisters. You may want to recite it softly, swiftly, high or low pitched, like someone with hiccups/ a cold, a nasal voice and so on. How would a famous personality or someone you know recite a tongue twister? It could be a politician, a film star, a sportsperson, a cricket commentator, a teacher or the principal of the school! Good luck.

WORD LISTS

A-Z of Days of the Week:

F	Friday
M	Monday
S	Saturday, Sunday
T	Thursday, Tuesday
W	Wednesday

A-Z of Months of the Year:

A	April, August
D	December
F	February
J	January, June, July
M	March, May
N	November
O	October
S	September

A-Z of Animals and Birds:

A	albatross, alligator, anaconda, ant, antelope
B	baboon, bat, bear, bee, beetle, bison, bug, butterfly
C	canary, cat, chameleon, cheetah, chicken, chimpanzee, cobra, cockroach, cow, crane, cricket, cricket, crocodile, crow, cuckoo
D	dalmatian, deer, dinosaur, dog, dolphin, donkey, dove, drake, duck
E	eagle, eel, egret, elephant, emu
F	falcon, firefly, fish, flamingo, flea, fly, fox, frog
G	gander, giraffe, goat, goose, gorilla, grasshopper, gull
H	hare, hawk, hedgehog, hen, hippopotamus, hog, horse, hummingbird, hyena
I	ibis, iguana
J	jackal, jaguar, jay, jelly fish, joey
K	kangaroo, kingfisher, kite, kitten, koala, kookaburra

L	ladybug, lamb, lemur, leopard, lice, lion, lizard, llama, lobster
M	macaw, meerkat, mongoose, monkey, moose, mosquito, moth, mouse, mussels
N	nightingale, nymph
O	orangutan, ostrich, otter, owl, ox, oyster
P	panda, panther, parakeet, parrot, peacock, pelican, penguin, pig, pigeon, piranha, porcupine, puma, puppy
Q	quail
R	rabbit, racoon, rat, rattlesnake, raven, reindeer, rhinoceros, robin, rooster
S	salamander, seal, sheep, slug, snail, snake, sparrow, stork, swallow, swan
T	tadpole, tiger, toad, tortoise, toucan, trout, turkey, turtle
U	urchin
V	viper, vulture
W	walrus, wasp, weasel, whale, whelk, wolf, wombat, woodchuck, woodpecker
X	x-ray fish
Y	yak
Z	zebra

A-Z of Fruits, Vegetables and Flowers:

A	apple, apricot, artichoke, asparagus, aster, aubergine, avocado
B	banana, blackberry, bluebells, blueberry, brinjal, broccoli, Brussels sprouts, buttercups
C	cabbage, canna, cantaloupe, carnation, carrot, cauliflower, celery, cherry, chilli, chrysanthemum, coconut, cranberry, cucumber, custard apple
D	daffodil, dahlia, daisy, dandelion, date, dragon fruit, durian
E	edelweiss, eggplant
F	fig, forget me not, freesia
G	garlic, gerbera, gherkin, ginger, gladioli, gladiolus, gooseberry, gourd, grapefruit, grapes, guava
H	hibiscus, horseradish
I	iceberg lettuce, iris
J	jackfruit, jalapenos, jasmine
K	kale, kiwi

L	lady finger, leek, lemon, lettuce, lilac, lily of the valley, lily, lychee,
M	magnolia, mango, marigold, melon, mimosa, morning glory, mulberry, mushroom, muskmelon
N	narcissus, nectarine
O	olive, onion, orange, orchid, oregano
P	pansy, papaya, parsley, passion fruit, peas, peach, peanut, pear, peony, pepper, periwinkle, pineapple, plum, poppy, potato, primrose, pumpkin
Q	quince
R	raspberry, rose
S	spinach, squash, strawberry, sunflower
T	tangerine, tuberose, tulip, turnip
U	ugli fruit
V	violet
W	water chestnut, watercress, watermelon, wood apple
Y	yam
Z	zucchini, zinnia

A-Z of Colours:

A	aquamarine
B	beige, black, blue, bronze, brown, burgundy
C	crimson
F	fawn
G	gold, green, grey
I	indigo
K	khaki
L	lavender, lilac
M	magenta, mahogany, maroon, mauve, mustard
O	orange
P	peach, pink, plum, purple
R	red
S	silver
T	turquoise
V	violet
W	white

Y	yellow

A-Z of Precious Stones:

A	amethyst
C	coral
D	diamond
E	emerald
G	garnet
J	jade
L	lapis lazuli
M	moonstone
O	onyx, opal
P	pearl
R	ruby
S	sapphire
T	topaz, turquoise

A-Z of Places:

A	Abu Dhabi, Allahabad, Argentina, Australia
B	Bahamas, Bangalore, Belgium, Brazil, Burma
C	Canada, Chennai, Chile, China
D	Damascus, Delhi, Denmark
E	Egypt
F	Fiji, Finland, France
G	Germany, Goa, Gujarat
H	Hawaii, Hungary
I	Iceland, India, Italy
J	Jaipur, Japan
K	Kashmir, Kathmandu, Kenya, Kolkata, Kula Lampur
L	Leh, Libya, London, Ludhiana
M	Maldives, Mali, Mangalore, Morocco, Mumbai, Mysore
N	Nagpur, Nepal, Norway
O	Oman, Ooty,
P	Patna, Pune, Peru, Poland
Q	Qatar, Queensland

R	Rome, Russia,
S	Singapore, Spain, Sweden, Switzerland
T	Thailand, Timbuktu, Turkey
U	U.A.E., Udaipur, U.K., U.S.A.
V	Varanasi, Venice, Vienna
W	Wales
Y	Yemen
Z	Zambia, Zimbabwe

A-Z of Names:

A	Aira, Alia, Angelina
B	Belinda, Brenda, Brian, Bobby
C	Cavery, Chris
D	Diana, Dino, Diya
E	Ed, Edgar, Elizabeth, Ellie
F	Fanny, Fiona, Flora, Frank
G	Gia, Gisele, Greta
H	Henry
I	Ida, Isha,
J	Jack, James, Jane, Janet, Jeanette, Jill
K	Kevin, Kia, Krish
L	Lara, Laura, Lavina, Leela, Lina, Lola
M	Meena, Meeta, Meeta, Molly, Myra
N	Nia, Nishi, Nita
O	Olga, Om,
P	Preesha, Priya, Polly
Q	Quasar
R	Ravi, Romeo, Rose
S	Sanaya, Selina, Serina, Shania
T	Tia, Tina, Tisha
U	Urvi,
V	Veronica, Victor
W	Wanda, Whitney
X	Xavier
Y	Yatin
Z	Zeenat

A-Z of Adjectives/ Describing words:

A	anxious, angry, agile, aloof, ace, acute, alarming, alike, all, angelic, aromatic, artistic, arty, avid, aristocratic, atrocious
B	bad, baked, bare, beautiful, best, better, big, bland. blind, blunt, blurry, boiled, bold, bored, boring, bossy, brave, breezy, brief, bright, broke, broken, bruised, burnt
C	calm, careless, caring, casual, catchy, chaotic, cheap, cheeky, cheerful, chic, clever, cloudy, clumsy, cluttered, cold, colourful, courageous, crackle, crazy, creamy, creepy, crisp, crude, crunchy, curious, cute
D	dainty, daring, dark, darling, dashing, deaf, dear, delicious, dotting, dreamy, droopy, drunk, dry, dusky, dusty
E	eager, easy, economical, edgy, edible, eerie, eldest, elusive, empty, entire, epic, every, evil, exact, excellent, exceptional, exciting, exclusive, extinct, extra, extravagant
F	faithful, fake, famous, fast, few, fiery, fit, flimsy, fluffy, foamy, forgetful, friendly, funny, furry
G	gaga, gaudy, gawky, gentle, ghastly, giant, gifted, gracious, great, greedy, grumpy
H	heavy, helpful, hopeless, horrible, hot, hungry, humungous, hypnotic, hysterical
I	icky, iconic, icy, idiotic, impatient, inky, insane, instant, intelligent, interesting, irrational, irritated, itchy
J	jarring, jazzy, jealous, jinxed, jittery, jovial, joyful, juicy, jumbo
K	kind, kindhearted, knotty, knowledgeable
L	lacy, lame, lanky, last, late, lazy, lazy, leaky, lean, least, left, legal, lethal, like, limp, local, lonely, long, lose, lost, loud, lovely, loyal, lucky
M	magical, many, marvellous, melodious, merry, meticulous, mischievous, mysterious
N	naïve, narrow, nasty, natty, naughty, needy, nervous, new, next, nice, nosy, nude, null, numb, nutritious
O	obese, obnoxious, obsessed, odd, oily, okay, old, only, opaque, open, ordinary, original, own
P	painful, pale, peaceful, pearly, peppery, peppy, pert, perky, petite, petty, piggy, playful, plump, plush, poky, polite, pointed, poor, pop, powerful, pretty, privy, proud, public,

	puffy, punk, puzzling
Q	quaint, quarrelsome, queer, quick, quiet, quintessential, quirky, quizzical
R	racy, rainy, rare, rare, ravishing, raw, real, recent, reclusive, regular, regular, repentant, repulsive, revengeful, rhyming, rhythmic, rich, ripe, rocky, rosy, rough, rowdy, royal, rude, rural, rustic
S	sad, safe, salty, sassy, scary, seasonal, selfish, sharp, shiny, shoddy, short, shy, sickly, silent, silky, silly, simple, sinful, single, skillful, sleek, slim, slippery, slow, slurred, sly, small, smart, smelly, sober, social, soft, soggy, solid, solo, some, sooty, sore, sour, spacey, speedy, spicy, spiked, spooky, springy, stale, stark, starved, steamed, stern, sticky, stiff, still, stolen, stout, straight, streaked, strict, striking, strong, stubborn, stunning, stupid, stylish, suave, subtle, svelte, sweet
T	talkative, tall, tasty, terrible terrific, terrifying, timid, tiny, tired, troubled, truthful
U	ugly, ultimate, unusual, useful, useless, usual, utmost
V	vague, vain, varied, victorious, violent, viral, vivacious, vivid, voracious, vulgar
W	wacky, warm, wary, watchful, wavy, weak, wet, whimsical, whole, wholesome, wicked, wild, wimpy, windy, witty, wobbly, wonderful, woody, worse, worst, wriggly
Y	yankee, young, youthful, yucky, yummy
Z	zealous, zestful, zigzag

A-Z of Numbers:

B	billion
C	century, crore
D	double, dozen
E	eight, eleven, eighteen, eighty, eighty- eight
F	four, five, fourteen, fifteen, forty, forty-four, forty-five, fifty, fifty-four, fifty-five
H	hundred
L	lac
M	million

N	nine, nineteen, ninety, ninety-nine
O	one
S	six, seven, sixteen, seventeen, sixty, sixty-six, sixty-seven, seventy, seventy- six, seventy- seven
T	two, three, ten, twelve, thirteen, twenty, twenty-two, twenty-three, thirty, thirty-two, thirty-three, thousand, ten thousand, trillion, twice, triple
Z	zillion

A-Z of Homophones and Homonyms:

A	air/ heir/err, allowed/ aloud, Ann/ an, as/ ass
B	bald/ bawled, ball/bawl, banned/ ban, Barry/ bury/ berry, bat, be/ bee, bear/ bare, bell, blue/ blew, Bob/ bob, bore/ boar, bowl, bust/ bused, by/buy/ bye
C	can, creek/ creak, crews/ cruise, Czech/ check
D	dear/ deer, desert/ dessert, dew/ due, dough/ door
E	ear/ year, eight/ ate, even, ewe/ you,
F	flee/ flea, flour/ flower, flu/ flew, fly, for/ four/ fore, fowl/foul
G	gait/ gate, Greece/ grease,
H	hail/ hale, hair/ hare, hear/ here, heard/ herd, horse/ hoarse
I	in/ inn
J	jam, jeans/ genes
K	kite, knew/ new/ gnu, knot/ not
L	lean, led/ lead, light,
M	made/ maid, main/ mane, male/ mail, Mary/ marry/merry, May/ may, mousse/moose,
N	need/ knead, night/ knight, nun/ none
O	one/ won, our/ hour
P	pail/ pale, pair/ pare/ pear, peace/ piece, praise/ prays/ preys, principal/ principle, profit/ prophet, punch
Q	queue/ cue
R	rain/ reign, red/ read, ring, road/ rowed, roll, rote/ wrote, row
S	sale/sail, scale, scene/ seen, scent/ sent, sea/ see, son/ sun, sort/ sought, soul/ sole, sow/sew, sum/ some, sweet/ suite
T	there/ they're, tide/ tied, tie, to/ too/ two, toast, trunk, tyre/

	tier,
U	urn/ earn
V	vain/ vein, verse/ worse
W	waste/ waist, wear/ where, week/ weak, whale/ wail, which/ witch, whole/ hole, width/ with, Will/ will, world/ whirled, would/wood, write/ right
Y	yoke/ yolk, your/ you're

A-Z of Alliterations:

A	agony aunt, amazing alliterations, army of ants
B	a bee in your bonnet, as blind as a bat, as bright as a button, as busy as a beaver, baby blues, backbiting, backbreaker, bad blood, ball and bat, bated breath, bear the brunt, beat around the bush, Beauty and the Beast, best buddies, bevy of beauties, big bucks, birthday boy, boils and blisters, bouncy ball, bread and butter, bunch of bananas, busy as a bee
C	cakes and cookies, cash crunch, chip chop, chit-chat, chocolate chips, caravan of camels, clutch of chicks, clutter of cats, cool as a cucumber, country club, crystal clear
D	as dead as a dodo, as dry as dust, as dull as a dishwasher, damsel in distress, daredevil, daydream, dead duck, dilly-dally, dime a dozen, ding dong, do or dare, do or die, doctors and dentists, down in the dumps
E	Easter eggs, electric eels
F	fame and fortune, farm fresh, farm to fork, fast and furious, fast or feast, fat to fit, fish and fries, fish fillet, flip-flop, forgive and forget, frequent flier, friends and foes, friends forever, from the frying pan to the fryer, fun and frolic
G	all that glitters is not gold, gaggle of geese, gentle giant, gift of the gab, go-getter, God-given gift, God is great, grass is greener, greengrocer
H	as hot as hell, hale and hearty, halfheartedly, hard-hearted, head over heels, heaven and hell, hip-hop, Horrible Henry, horses and hooves
I	insult to injury
J	Jack and Jill, jams and jellies, jumbo jet, jump with joy, jumping jacks

K	King Kong, knick-knack
L	larger than life, laughing out loud, laundry list, law of the land, learning to love to learn, like it or leave it, live/ love/ laugh, look before you leap, lost in love, love letter
M	making a mountain out of a molehill, measles and mums, method to the madness, Mickey and Minnie, mind over matter, mix and match, money matters, more the merrier
N	naughty or nice, no news, now or never
O	odd one out, over and out
P	as proud as peacock, pain and pleasure, paper and pen, part and parcel, peer pressure, pen pal, Peter Pan, picture perfect, pied piper, pile of papers, ping pong, pitter- patter, pocketful of posies, pod of peas, pots and pans, practice makes perfect, prim and proper, pudding and pie, push and pull
Q	quietly quit
R	rags to riches, rant and rave, Richie Rich, ring a ring a roses, road rage, roadside Romeos, rock and roll, round robin
S	as smooth as silk, safe and sound, shimmer and shine, shoes and socks, shoe-shine, shopping spree, short and sweet speech, simple Simon, sing-song, sink or swim, slow and steady, slow as a snail, soup for the soul, spic and span, spoilt sport, sugar and spice, sun and sand, swan song, sweet and salty, sweet and sour, sweet as sugar, sweet sixteen, sweet smell of success
T	it takes two to tango, table for two, tangy tomato, tasty treats, temper tantrums, terrible teens, testing times, thick and thin, tic tack toe, tick- tock, time and tide, tip toe, tip top, tit for tat, tongue-tied, tongue twisters, top ten, tough times, travel tales, trials and tribulations, trick or treat, tricks of the trade, tried and tested, turn the tables, twin towers
V	vice-versa, vis- a- vis
W	warm weather woollens, warp and weft, Wee Willie Winkie, war of words, weeping willow, where there is a will there is a way, wishy-washy, wit and wisdom, wonders of the world
Y	yin yang
Z	zigzag

TONGUE TWISTER GRAPHIC ORGANISER TEMPLATE

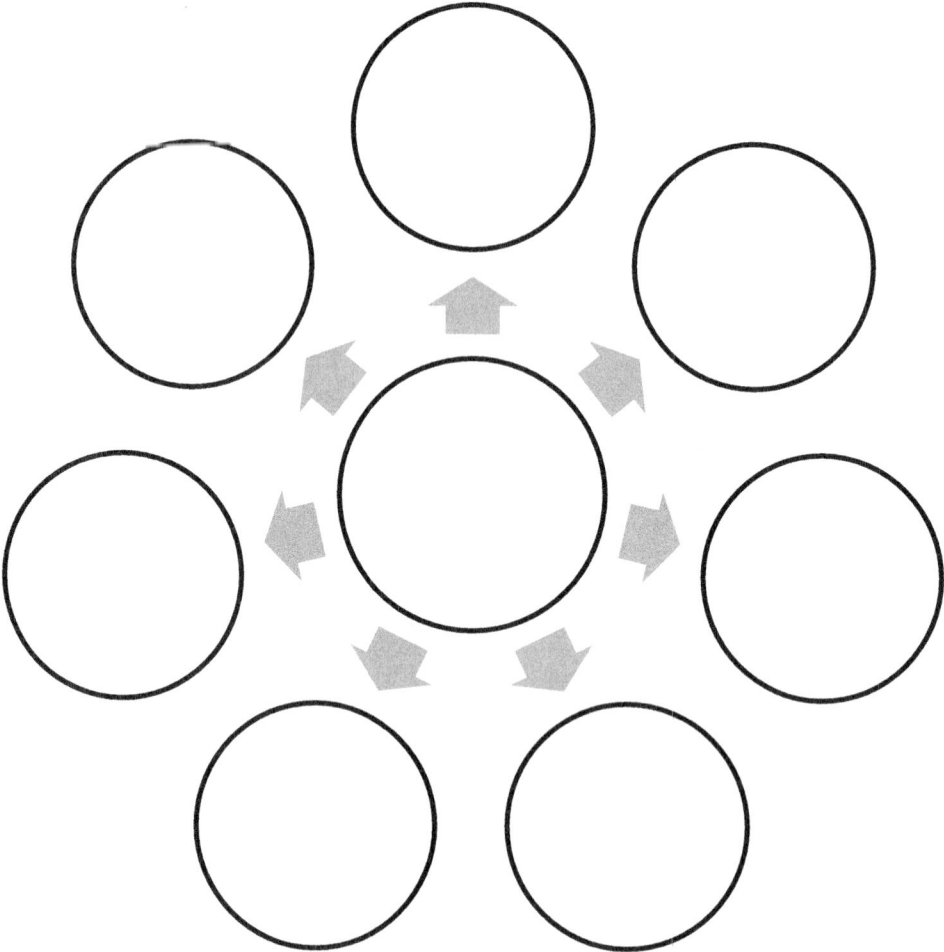

Tongue Twister:

_____

MY TONGUE TWISTERS LIST

A	
B	
C	
D	
E	
F	
G	
H	
I	
J	
K	
L	
M	
N	
O	
P	
Q	
R	
S	
T	
U	
V	
W	
X	
Y	
Z	

MY WALL OF FAME

Write your favourite tongue twisters in the stars.

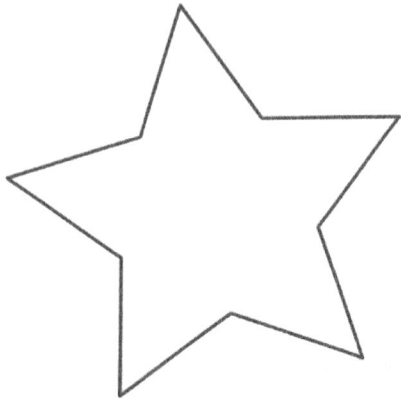

Printed in Great Britain
by Amazon

60187499R00037